Shared Value in SMEs
Evidence from Europe

Roland Berberich

Legal Information

© / Copyright: 2017 Roland Berberich

First Edition

Coverdesign, Ilustration: Roland Berberich
Publisher: Roland Berberich

Printed by CreateSpace in various locations

ISBN Paperback: 9781545520291

This work and its parts are protected by copyright. Any use without prior agreement from author or publisher is prohibited. This includes but is not limited to (electronic) copying, translation and distribution.

References should be made with the following, information:

Berberich, R., 2017. Shared Value in SMEs: Evidence from Europe, Roland Berberich, Printed by CreateSpace - An Amazon.com Company

Foreword by the Autor

This piece of work is an edited version of my 2013 Master thesis 'Can SMEs create Shared Value'. I have taken the original, edited obvious errors and brought it into a more readable format. No new date out or analysis was added.

The concept of shared value, 'monetising social responsibility', has been around much longer than Porter and Kramer's (2011) suggestion. In fact, one of the arguments of my thesis has been that the concept has been the actual starting point of CSR and through years of development the phenomenon has 'come full circle'.

When factory owners during the Industrial Revolution started building affordable accommodation for their workforce they did not only address a pressing social need. By offering better living standards they attracted and retained the resource essential for their own business success. Years later Henry Ford had a similar idea, paying his workers more than his competitors and thus contributing to the rise of the Ford Motor Corporation.

The idea of social responsibility certainly has seen remarkable development and current social reality suggests the continued need for going the extra mile for those that can afford to help those who can't. Globalisation and (social) media have increased the penetrative ability of 'needs' to become visible for a larger crowd. Bringing perceived problems to the attention of a global audience arguably increases the chances of a solution. Indeed multinational corporations (MNCs) have started to set up remarkable CSR programs for various reasons and with different results.

While large corporations have the advantage of resource abundance, the majority of businesses in many countries are still small to medium-sized (SMEs). CSR has not only since the so-called financial crisis (2008 onward) been a financial and organisational impossibility for SMEs but their perceived shortcomings concerning size and location make it almost impossible for them to achieve recognisable impact. Moreover, how could an SME already struggling because of a lack of resources acquire and channel additional time and money into a social responsibility program without directly measurable (financial) return?

Shared value as a way of monetising these efforts should be the ideal solution for SMEs experiencing increasing public scrutiny from a global audience urging corporations to 'do good'. By making instead of costing money it could attract more small businesses to meet the mandate of social responsibility through a value proposition with the aim to address social needs, prospering while helping society. The sheer number of SMEs suggests, while individual impact may be limited, on a grand scale the results could be tremendous.

During and since this research project I have yet to meet a single business person that entirely rejects the concept, although some businesses argue charities to be better suited for that kind of work. Focusing on business the firm could and should contribute to society through value propositions and 'paying their taxes'. This also shows that the understanding of CSR is still somewhat lacking. 'Doing good' is not a good enough explanation any more and unbeknownst to the firm those aforementioned charities suffer the same financial constraints as do governments and NGOs.

Activating a larger number of businesses would alleviate the limited reach the individual firm has and by sheer numbers create the desired results. This implies that CSR needs to be explained beyond the charity notion, a problem perhaps coming from the 37 definitions (Dahlsrud, 2008) of CSR and a lack of connectivity between SMEs among themselves but also with larger businesses and NGOs.

I believe this research has shown that SMEs are more than capable of creating an impact in the world of CSR and that continuing deficits make it impossible for them to achieve their potential. Several suggestions are made towards the end of this thesis to address the remaining problems so that a globalised CSR can benefit its audience and creators.

Preface

The economy still in turmoil of the financial crisis and recession has left many companies struggling while the capitalistic system itself is being questioned (Porter and Kramer, 2011; Rappaport, 2011). Several ways to amend the system and ways to rekindle the economy are being suggested and explored and Creating Shared Value (CSV) could be one of these measures to improve the situation. Thus the research investigates the feasibility of small and medium businesses (SMEs) engaging in CSV.

The majority of business entities in Europe are small businesses thus the study aims to assess if and how SMEs could create shared value, investigate the difficulty and benefits of such attempt. Furthermore it explores whether implementation of CSV is successful by assessing aims and outcomes and finally to raise the awareness of CSV in SMEs.

In the current economic situation and with public demand for increased social responsibility of corporations, CSV could offer SMEs the possibility to fulfil these obligations in a fashion that suits their constrained resources. Owners being deeply involved in daily business do neither have the time nor the financial resources to engage in pure reputation oriented corporate social responsibility (CSR) programmes. Thus uniting the need for social responsibility and the imperative to create value could offer the possibility to address both needs at the same time.

Data was gathered by ten semi-structured qualitative interviews with owners of ten small businesses and analysed to understand the feasibility of CSV in SMEs. It was discovered that all research participants were willing to implement such policies but mostly unable to do so. Difficulties such as financial constraints but also benefits as the possibility to gain competitive advantage were discovered. SME owners are unaware of policymakers' efforts which make existing structures seem inefficient at communicating. Owners' perception and motivation are crucial factors for implementation of these policies and what shape these efforts take.

Findings suggest re-uniting CSR and CSV to allow for a more flexible approach of implementation and consequently expanded prevalence. Existing structures should be fully utilised or changed according to need so SMEs can be reached by policymakers. More small organisations then could adopt social responsibility into their daily operations and with their combined impact lead the economy out of the crisis.

Table of Contents

Foreword by the Autor 5

1. Introduction 13
2. Literature Review 15
   2.1. SMEs 16
   2.2. The concept of CSV 18
      2.2.1. Timeline of CSR 19
      2.2.2. "The Pyramid of CSR" 19
      2.2.3 World Business Council for Sustainable Development CSR Definition.20
      2.2.4. Origin and Evolution of CSR – Industrial Revolution to the 1990s 21
      2.2.5. The 1990s onward – Globalisation 22
      2.2.6. CSV in SMEs – The solution? 23
3. Research Methodology 25
   3.1. Overview 25
      3.1.1. Research Objectives 26
   3.2. Research Strategy 26
      3.2.1. Collection and Analysis of Qualitative Data 28
      3.2.2. The Qualitative Approach 28
      3.2.3. Semi Structured Interviews 29
      3.2.4. Research Sample and Sampling Method 30
   3.3. Data Analysis 31
   3.4. Ethical considerations 33
   3.5. Data Validity 33
   3.6. Limitations of the Research and Addressing them 34
   3.7. Summary of Research Design 34
4. Findings and Discussion 35
   4.1. Chapter Overview 35
   4.2. Summary of Research Sample 35
   4.3. Finding 1: Awareness and Perception of CSR and CSV 38
      4.3.1. Awareness and Implementation Criteria - Owners as Decisive Factor ..39

4.4. Finding 2: Motivation for (Non-)implementation	**41**
4.4.1. Philosophy, education or culture	43
4.5. Finding 3: Difficulties, Benefits and Successes	**43**
4.5.1. Financial and organisational constraints	45
4.5.2. Guidance and Support – The Role of Policymakers	46
4.5.3. Confusing versions of CSR and CSV – Uniting definitions	47
4.5.4. Successful CSV	48
4.5.5. Benefits of Implementation	49
4.6. Summary of Findings	**51**
5. Conclusions and Suggestions	**53**
5.1. Overview	53
5.2. Conclusions	53
5.3. Suggestions and Recommendations	54
6. Reference	**57**

List of figures

Figure 1: 'The pyramid of CSR', Source: Carroll (1991, p. 42)   p.20
Figure 2: 'Research strategies, questions and purposes',
      Source: Blaikie (2009, p. 105)   p. 27
Figure 3: 'The process of inductive analysis', Source: Shaw (1999)   p. 32
Figure 4: Overview of research sample   p.37

Date conventions
All dates are in the format DD.MM.YYYY

1. Introduction

This research has been conducted as a part of an MSc study in 'Strategic Project Management' at Heriot Watt University, Edinburgh, Scotland. An insight to whether or not SMEs could implement the concept of CSV successfully is perceived to be overdue.

SMEs are considered the 'backbone of the economy' (Wymenga et al., 2012, p. 9) and in recent years have received more attention from both policymakers as well as researchers. CSR and CSV are argued to be concepts that could address various economic and social issues of the world today (Durmaz et al., 2011; Midttun et al., 2006; Porter and Kramer, 2011). The concept of CSV was introduced in 2006 and although the lack of research concerning SMEs has been criticised (Karnani, 2007), the perceived gap has not been addressed. Additionally the related concept of CSR has only started to be researched within an SME context (Castka et al., 2004; Kechiche and Soparnot, 2012).

Therefore this study aims to explore if and how SMEs could utilise the concept of CSV, the outcomes of such implementation and the difficulties and benefits SMEs are experiencing when engaging in the creation of shared value. Forming the majority of businesses in Europe and the USA this large number of organisations' business potential and impact cannot be emphasised enough. Whereas Porter and Kramer (2011) already argue CSV to release a new wave of innovation and prosperity it is understood that society as such would massively profit from the economy as a whole utilising this concept. Increasing prosperity on a global scale is argued to be beneficial for societal development (Wilkinson and Pickett, 2010).

Relevant literature is reviewed in chapter two, to highlight origin and current state of academic discourse in CSR and CSV. It is considered vital to understand origin and development of CSR including its evolving into CSV. The historic role of CSR in the economy enables to gain an insight how CSR and CSV could create impact and improve economic performance. The following discussion of methodology elaborates on philosophy, data collection methods and general design of the study. Interpretivism as a philosophy and qualitative semi-structured interviews conducted with an overall inductive framework are perceived to offer key advantages when investigating small businesses. A qualitative study depends on meaning rather than numbers and figures and to answer the research questions it is imperative to grasp the meaning, the opinions and motivation of the research participants.

The result of these interviews is presented and discussed in the fourth chapter. CSV in SMEs depends on a number of criteria which will be the focus through said chapter. Overall it was found that CSV can be successfully implemented by SMEs – very similar to the findings of previous studies on CSR in SMEs. Furthermore a discussion about the differentiation of CSR and CSV will offer a possibility to re-unite both concepts.

The fifth and final chapter summarises findings, draws conclusions and offers suggestions to improve the success rate of SMEs engaging in CSV. Economic potential is lost by SMEs that despair before even trying to utilize the potential CSV could have for them – which is not surprising when concerning the inadequate knowledge transfer from policymakers and academia down to business owners.

2. Literature Review

This research focuses on small to medium sized enterprises (SMEs) as they form a majority in the economy regarding many aspects (Basefsky and Sweeney, 2006; Federation of Small businesses, 2013; Forum Europe, 2012). It intends to explore if and how SMEs apply the concept of creating shared value (CSV) in order to assume their corporate social responsibility (CSR). Initially a brief introduction on SMEs is given highlighting some strengths and challenges for SMEs in the current economic environment. It is argued that SMEs are facing several difficulties and that implementation of CSR is one of them (Lepoutre and Heene, 2006). Further it is argued that CSR is no longer optional but mandatory (Smith, 2003).

The following section introduces the concept of creating shared value (CSV). It is argued that CSV is an evolution of CSR, yet fundamentally different from it, coming from a different intention (Porter and Kramer, 2011). Porter and Kramer (2011) further argue CSV to be superseding CSR as it aims at business success, thus accommodating Friedman's (1972) argument as well as acknowledging wider responsibilities of the business.

To understand the link to CSR a brief history and timeline of the concept is given. The idea of CSR can be traced back to the advent of the modern organisation during the industrial revolution (Crane et al., 2008, pp. 19–46). Urbanisation, for example, as a result of agricultural population moving to the cities to find work, created a series of issues, particulrly housing (Engels, 2009) shall be mentioned in more depth.

The "globalist hypothesis" (Gjolberg, 2009, p. 607) argues that recent change such as globalisation has left a "governance gap" (ibid). Further it is argued that organisations are expected to fill this gap particularly as they have been profiting from it and through several actions became detached from society (Porter et al., 2012). CSR could be argued to reconcile this relationship by giving back to society through creation of shared value (CSV). A good relationship with society is perceived to be of outmost importance following the concept of "social license to operate" (Boutilier et al., 2011; Pike, 2012; Sklair, 2001). CSR has become mandatory and organisations are urged to find ways implementing it in order to survive.

Particularly SMEs can be argued to struggle finding a way to accommodate. Partly due to special circumstances (Lepoutre and Heene, 2006) in the nature of SMEs but also due to economic reasons (Duan et al., 2009; Steen, 2013). As CSR is mandatory and not a voluntary exercise a new approach should be sought to accommodate both the need for implementing CSR but also the special circumstances of the firm.

Finally it is argued that CSV in SMEs could potentially solve the problem for these companies to fulfil their perceived CSR obligations. It is argued that CSV aims directly at value creation whereas CSR requires investment of time and money, two resources that SMEs cannot easily access. Finance in particular is a major concern (Duan et al., 2009) and the dominating position of owners in many SMEs leaves little time for non-revenue creating activities (Nooteboom, 1993, p. 288). Hence a revenue creating process that allows flexible implementation is needed in order to accommodate the situation SMEs find themselves in. Limited research is available on how SMEs implement CSR (Castka et al., 2004; European Commission, 2013a; Karnani, 2007) and concerning shared value SMEs have been studied solely as recipients, being developed by a large company (MARS, 2013; Nestle, 2012a, 2013; Williams and Hayes, 2013).

While CSR implementation in SMEs has been researched to some extent there is currently no similar study concerning the concept of CSV although this gap in research has been criticized (Karnani, 2007). The attention and focus on SMEs given by the European Commission and associated bodies (European Commission, 2002, 2005, 2013a) has also given rise in the number of academic research focusing on SMEs. Particularly concerning CSR in SMEs there has been a number of studies (Castka et al., 2004; Ciliberti et al., 2008; European Commission, 2013a). Summarizing the available research it can be stated that implementation of CSR is facing difficulties in SME, yet is possible if the nature of SMEs is accommodated. As stated before, the owner in small businesses has a very central and time consuming role in daily operations (Nooteboom, 1993, p. 288). Financial limitations (Beck and Demirguc-Kunt, 2006; Duan et al., 2009; Steen, 2013) further demand an approach to CSR that rather creates revenue than cost money.

2.1. SMEs

Small to medium sized enterprises (SMEs) are increasingly regarded as vital for local and economic development (Kotey and Meredith, 1997; Neck et al., 2003). They *'are an essential source of jobs, create entrepreneurial spirit and innovation in the EU and are thus crucial for fostering competitiveness and employment'* (European Commission, 2005, p. 3). Being recognised as essential assets (BMWi, 2012; European Commission, 2005; Kotey and Meredith, 1997; Neck et al., 2003) further research on SMEs should be considered and is argued for (Tansky and Heneman, 2003).

SMEs currently make up more than 99 % of business entities across the EU (Forum Europe, 2012) whereas in the UK the figure is 99.9 % in 2012 and the corresponding figure for the US in 2005 was 99.7 % (Basefsky and Sweeney, 2006). In 2012 the typical SME would be classed as a Micro Enterprise even (European Commission, 2005) and statistically employ 4.22 people (Wymenga et al., 2012, p. 15). Data for the USA in 2008 (US Census Bureau, 2008) shows a total of 27.7 million firms with over 120.6 million employees resulting in 4.34 employees per business. Hence it can be argued the "average" company is not only an SME but a Micro Enterprise with less than 10 people.

Definitions of what exactly an SME is vary to some extent and for the purpose of this research the definition of the European Commission (2005, p. 51) will be employed. It states that an SME has a headcount smaller than 250 employees and either an annual turnover of less than 50 million € or an annual balance sheet total of less than 43 million € (European Commission, 2005, p. 14). Further explanations are given in the same paper to determine how these figures are to be calculated. While most SMEs are small, local businesses they are also deeply rooted in the local community. Whatever discerning argument is used, it is generally argued that SMEs are "the backbone of the economy" (BMWi, 2012).

However, it also must be acknowledged that SMEs could be disadvantaged in other aspects; the difficulty in acquiring finance for example (Duan et al., 2009; Steen, 2013) which hampers growth (Beck and Demirguc-Kunt, 2006) and the difficulty to engage in CSR due to size as well as financial constraints and lack of time (Lepoutre and Heene, 2006). Duan et al (2009) argue that SMEs are facing disadvantages when compared to larger enterprises mainly because of high transaction costs, information asymmetry, credit filtration and high risk (Duan et al., 2009, p. 73). For banks, larger loans incur the same transaction cost and are thus preferred, leaving SMEs struggling to meet collateral demands as to secure the borrowing and banks are reluctant to lend money to SMEs when statistical data shows more than half of SMEs to fail within four years of their existence (ibid).

In most SMEs the owners are also running the daily operations or are at least deeply involved, leaving no time to properly coordinate or even engage in CSR efforts (Ciliberti et al., 2008, p. 1579; Nooteboom, 1993, p. 288). Therefore any attempt to fulfil obligations concerning CSR must be accommodating the situation SMEs find themselves in if these attempts shall not fail. The existence and extent of CSR obligations will be explored in the section covering the evolution of CSR since the 1990s. It is argued that CSR is mandatory for any kind of business and that implementation is a matter of approach (European Commission, 2013a; Smith, 2003).

2.2. The concept of CSV

Creating shared value (CSV) has been argued to be superior to purely reputation driven CSR (Porter and Kramer, 2011, p. 65). The concept was first introduced by Porter (Porter and Kramer, 2006) and has since been expanded (2012; 2011), studied by other academia (Williams and Hayes, 2013) but also criticised (Karnani, 2007).

CSV is defined as a connection of *'societal and economic progress'* (Porter and Kramer, 2011, p. 65) and is argued to spark *'the next wave of global growth'* (ibid). Companies can utilize this approach in three ways:

1. Reconceiving products and markets: Rethinking market strategies to meet the needs of the existing markets and accessing new markets by redesigning products. Often argued is to serve *'the bottom of the pyramid'* (Prahalad and Hart, 2002). Additionally the new approach could lead to lower production or supply cost. Adidas in partnership with Grameen Bank started offering low cost shoes to the poor in Bangladesh. Thus a new market was accessed with a branded product and created shared value by lowering health cost (Klein, 2011).

2. Redefining productivity in the value chain: Modifications in the value chain can reduce cost and boost productivity. Walmart for example lowered carbon emissions by improving delivery routes and redesigning packaging, thus saving 200 Million $ although the number of shipments increased (Porter and Kramer, 2011, p. 69).

3. Enabling local cluster development: Working together closely with suppliers to improve their skills can also pay off with a more secure and reliably supply chain. Of example may be the developments in the Moga Milk district, spurred by Nestles investments and skill transfer (Nestle, 2012a, p. 131, 2012b) and engagement with rural coffee planters in Africa and Latin America (Porter and Kramer, 2011, p. 70). As a result Ivorian farmers increased their income by 300 %. Moving quality control directly to the point of origin for example allowed Nestle to pay premium prices directly to the growers, yet offer an affordable premium product to the customer (ibid).

Apparently the supply chain becomes a major item in creating shared value. The supply chain is modified from a business point of view yet the impact of these modifications goes beyond saving cost. In summary it could be stated that CSV is utilizing CSR to leverage business success directly. The possibility of such a targeted approach has been researched and confirmed (Bhattacharya, 2011). Although CSV is a relatively new concept it has been criticised (Karnani, 2007) particularly for focussing on large multinational companies. Karnani argues smaller companies to be better suited to serve the poor and thus create shared value (ibid, p. 96).

Research is almost exclusively done via case studies (Klein, 2011; Porter et al., 2012; Williams and Hayes, 2013) and often only mention financial benefits. It is argued that not all, particularly the societal benefits, can be fully grasped (Porter et al., 2012). The concept spurs the questions how the value creation process can be optimised in such way as to create benefits for a variety of stakeholders including the society as a whole. Further it raises the question what non-financial benefits are created. To understand and widen the concept of CSV and to show its link with CSR the following section will give a brief timeline of CSR.

2.2.1. Timeline of CSR

This section will explore the definition and development of the concept of CSR. The idea of CSR has become widely popular during the last few decades often without a proper definition as to what exactly CSR is about. No less than 27 authors have offered 37 definitions (Dahlsrud, 2008) of the concept leaving much room for interpretation. Lack of accepted framework (ibid) often leads to biased interpretations (van Marrewijk, 2003) fitting solely the observed situation and corporate entity. A widely acknowledged definition is *'The Pyramid of CSR'* (Carroll, 1991). Furthermore the World Business Council for Sustainable Development offers a more open view on CSR (Holme and Watts, 2000). It should be acknowledged that even without a consensus on definition (McWilliams et al., 2006, p. 8) the case for CSR is valid and strong (Carroll and Shabana, 2010).

2.2.2. "The Pyramid of CSR"

Carroll's "Pyramid of CSR" (1991, 1999) identifies four layers of responsibilities for the corporation. Inevitably this also visually attaches a ranking of these responsibilities although Carroll (1999) strongly argues these obligations need to be fulfilled in their entirety and at all times. Economic responsibilities form the foundation upon which the remaining three responsibilities rest. The second layer being legal responsibilities while ethical responsibilities form the third and philanthropic responsibilities the top layer of the pyramid.

Economic and legal responsibilities are absolute and cannot be constantly violated or the organisation will cease to exist. The third layer describes the ethical responsibility to act fair and exceed the minimum legal standards set by the second layer (Visser, 2006). Whereas fulfilment of these three layers is to varying degree demanded from society, philanthropy is voluntary, yet desired (Müller and Schaltegger, 2008, p. 56) to exceed societal expectations. As ethical standards are not codified and, moreover vary across cultures (Wines and Napier, 1992) and over time, the firm must change with its surrounding.

Figure 1: The Pyramid of CSR

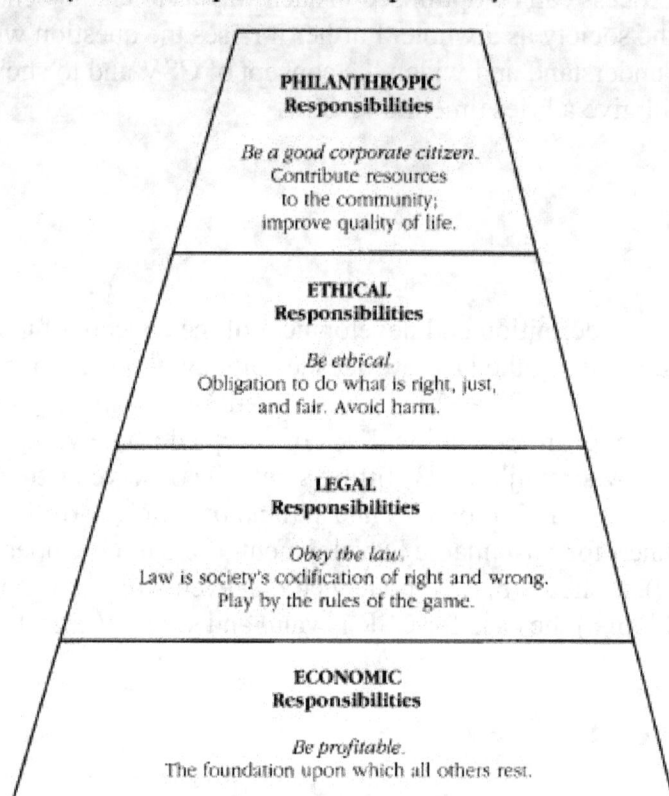

Source: Carroll (1991, p. 42)

2.2.3 World Business Council for Sustainable Development CSR Definition

The definition by the world business council was first mentioned in 1998 and has been slightly modified into its current form. '*Corporate social responsibility is the continuing commitment by business to behave ethically and contribute to economic development while improving the quality of life of the workforce and their families as well as of the local community and society at large*' (Holme and Watts, 2000, p. 8).

This definition stresses that CSR is not a one off action and aims to contribute towards better living quality for society. According to Dahlsrud (2008) only another, similar definition by the Commission of European Communities is more widely spread. The definition does not offer a valuation or different levels of responsibilities. It highlights the need for organisations to take responsibility for a number of stakeholders and society.

Although simple, it incorporates a wide interpretation of possibilities how to implement the notion of CSR successfully into the business. Being very broad and open the organisation therefore gains more than one option how to implement CSR successfully. Considering the peculiarities of SMEs (Ciliberti et al., 2008, p. 1579), such as lack of resources and heavy involvement of the owners in daily business activities (Ciliberti et al., 2008, p. 1579; Nooteboom, 1993, p. 288), flexibility of implementation could be regarded as highly desirable. For the purpose of this research the definition by Holme and Watts shall be employed.

2.2.4. Origin and Evolution of CSR – Industrial Revolution to the 1990s

CSR is not a new concept, besides growing in importance over the last decades. As early as the industrial revolution factory owners were concerned about their workforce and their wellbeing, leading not only to employer driven regulations about health and safety but also voluntary improvements e.g. cheap and free accommodation for the workforce (Grollmann, 1996). Hence changes in work, the change of skill profiles and centralisation of work, among others, have led to social changes and continue to do so.

It is argued that living standards in England particularly housing had been improved by 1844 (Engels, 2009). Examples are the designed worker villages (e.g. Saltaire) in UK or 'mining colonies' in Germany (Grollmann, 1996; Smith, 2003; Vonde, 2012). Such effort solved the problem of accommodation for an increasing and centralised workforce. It could be argued that factory owners assumed a quasi patriarchic position, increasing obedience and productivity among the workers in return (Vonde, 2012). If the notion of increasing productivity had been more central in the argument these efforts could easily be classed as a first attempt of CSV.

Modern discourse on CSR arguably started in the 1950s with Bowen (1953). Yet there has been arguments that CSR is not necessary (Friedman, 1972) or even dangerous (Levitt, 1958). Social legislation from the 1870s onward (in Germany) and post WW II economic success may have reduced the immediate focus on CSR and still research expanded particularly since the 1960s (Carroll, 1999, p. 270). While the 1970s expanded on possible definitions of and approaches to CSR the 1980s then saw fewer attempts on definitions but opened new themes (ibid, p. 84). In summary it can be argued that the concept has enjoyed various degrees of appreciation and topics in CSR have changed over time. Still there is no universal definition (Dahlsrud, 2008; McWilliams et al., 2006, p. 8) though this argued to be of lesser importance (Carroll and Shabana, 2010).

2.2.5. The 1990s onward – Globalisation

Arguably the discussion on CSR has gained momentum through the increasing speed of globalisation (Gjolberg, 2009, p. 607). 'Globalist hypothesis' argues that increasing openness and interactions of formerly separated markets have led to trade-offs caused by the actions of the market participants and have led to a "governance gap" (ibid, pp.607,608) which should be addressed. CSR attempts to fill the gap where responsibilities are perceived to have shifted from governments to organisations (ibid). It is argued that while organisations have enjoyed greater liberties they should also take up greater responsibilities – *'Noblesse oblige'* (Duc de Lévis', 1808).

Further, corporate scandals (Gjolberg, 2009, p. 608) have led to anti-corporate and anti-globalisation sentiments that need addressing. Companies like Shell (Brech, 1995; Die WELT, 1995) or Apple (BBC, 2013; Garside, 2012) among others violated their perceived obligations towards society, resulting in further criticism and financial consequences. The recent horsemeat scandal in the UK in particular has raised concerns that companies are irresponsible and not 'appropriately punished' for their wrongdoing (Lawrence, 2013). When in the past it was sufficient to follow the law these events increasingly show that companies need to go beyond minimum effort and do what is perceived right. Even more it is argued that these societal demands outweigh legal requirements (Waddel, 2000, p. 38). The firm needs a "social license" to operate (Sklair, 2001).

Hence it could be argued that CSR is a direct response to these concerns, anti-corporate sentiments and against critics of Globalisation itself (Gjolberg, 2009, p. 608). In consequence implementing CSR would then be in the self-interest and to the benefit of the organisation (ibid). Further, the 'business case for CSR' has long since been discussed and accepted to result in various improvements for the organisation such as a better risk management, brand image and employee relations to name only three (Elkington and Fennell, 2000; Newell, 2000; Vogel, 2005; Waddel, 2000).

If CSR is accepted to be a response towards the anti-globalisation movement then it could be argued only to be necessary for globalised corporations (Gjolberg, 2009, p. 608). Yet other research suggests implementing CSR is no longer optional regardless of firm size (Cummings, 2012; Smith, 2003; TIME Magazine, 2012) but mandatory for any organisation especially when concerned with the notion of 'social license'.

With CSR no longer being optional, organisations need to find a way to live up to society's expectations, facing investment of time and money without immediate financial rewards, as CSR is argued to focus on reputation rather than revenue (Porter and Kramer, 2011, p. 76). This could be detrimental whenever resources are scarce. Particularly SMEs rather *'informal and intuitive'* approach (European Commission, 2013a) is at stake when concerned with peculiarities and economic imperfections (Baden et al., 2009; Ciliberti et al., 2008; Duan et al., 2009; European Commission, 2013a; Forum Europe, 2012; Nooteboom, 1993, p. 38; Steen, 2013). The reasons for underachieving society's expectations are irrelevant for critics that argue 'not whether, but how' SMEs could implement CSR (Smith, 2003). Hence a different approach towards CSR is needed, one that accommodates market imperfections and special circumstances of an organisation.

2.2.6. CSV in SMEs – The solution?

As stated above CSR is no longer optional for any organisation, especially when following Porter's arguments (2012, pp. 67, 68) why organisations face the duty of giving back to society. There will be circumstances where CSR is not an applicable approach due to financial constraints or lack of time. A direct approach that not only fulfils the perceived obligations of the organisation but also accommodates the particular situation that an organisation experiences at that given moment is needed.

Here CSV could supersede CSR as it creates value by leveraging CSR for business success (Bhattacharya, 2011). CSR then becomes detached from constrained budgets (Porter and Kramer, 2011, p. 76) and thus easier to implement. Further it accommodates Friedman's (1972) argument that profits are paramount. As argued by Porter (2012) the measurement of social benefits may be difficult but they are certainly apparent in the various case studies in the field. If SMEs could engage to deliver CSV their enormous business capacity and market penetration could leverage immense benefits for society. In summary one could state that a broader engagement in CSV could speed up the development of a more equal society, something that is argued to be beneficial for all (Wilkinson and Pickett, 2010).

3. Research Methodology

3.1. Overview

The study is using an inductive approach, which aims to *'establish descriptions of characteristics and patterns'* (Blaikie, 2009, p. 85). Probably being among the early studies in the field it intends to explore awareness and feasibility of CSV in SMEs. In order to understand these, it is deemed necessary to look at the motivation of business owners for their actions and to explore their activities. Therefore, data was collected through conducting semi-structured interviews with SME owners, supplemented by studying SMEs' documents in order to assess the possibility of SMEs engaging in CSV and to explore what difficulties and benefits can be encountered in the process of implementation.

It is acknowledged that the study has certain limitations, but these reflect commonly discussed weaknesses of the chosen data collection methods (Denscombe, 2007; Gomm, 2004; Patton, 2002, pp. 40–41) and will be addressed in the appropriate sections. However, as previous studies concerning CSV have been limited on MNCs and mostly used quantitative methods, a different approach towards shared value should be attempted to broaden the concept.

These limitations have been criticised (Karnani, 2007; Porter et al., 2012) and thus this study is conducted focussing on SMEs and qualitative data. Using semi-structured interviews is perceived to be suitable to assess SME owners' motivations as it enables the researcher to do in-depth exploration while helping understanding the impact. The advantages the chosen design is perceived to offer (Gomm, 2004) will also be discussed.

After outlining the research objectives the approach of the study will be discussed in more detail. Additionally the research sample's impact will be highlighted, as it is crucial for the data collection method. The imperatives and advantages of the chosen design will be explored in more detail before the limitations of the study will be addressed.

3.1.1. Research Objectives

The research has the following objectives:

1. Explore if and how SMEs utilize the concept of CSV.
2. Understand the difficulties SMEs face when engaging in CSV and the benefits they can create.
3. Investigate if CSV implementation is successful by assessing the intention of the owner and the perceived impact.
4. Raise awareness of CSR and CSV in SMEs.

3.2. Research Strategy

This study will utilise a qualitative approach, conducting semi-structured interviews supplemented by available documents, namely the websites of research participants. It is perceived that this design is suitable to achieve the research objective. Similar to other studies that explore new territory, this research will be conducted to assess feasibility of SMEs engaging in CSV and as such aims to justify further research in that matter.

Therefore this study will explore if the concept of CSV can be implemented by SMEs. The inductive approach has been selected in order to explore if and how SMEs can create shared value. This approach is usually chosen for exploration (Blaikie, 2009, p. 105, Table 4.2) to establish *'elementary descriptions'* (ibid, p. 83). Although not constituting a universal truth, the approach can establish a general understanding of social phenomena and patterns of association (ibid). In other words this study cannot answer all questions concerning CSV in SMEs but also is not intended to do so. Moreover the *'elementary description'* (ibid) suggests the task to be rather the verification of a general possibility of SMEs being able to use the concept.

Figure 2: 'Research strategies, questions and purposes'

Purpose	Research Strategy				Type of Research Questions
	Inductive	Deductive	Retroductive	Abductive	
Exploration	***			***	What
Description	***			***	What
Explanation	*	***	***		Why
Prediction	**	***			What
Understanding				***	Why
Change		*	**	**	How
Evaluation	**	**	**	**	What and Why
Assess Impacts	**	**	**	**	What and Why

Key: *** = major activity; ** = moderate activity; *minor activity. These 'weightings' of the connections between objectives and research strategies are indicative only.

Source: Blaikie (2009, p. 105)

Here the inductive approach has been chosen to explore if and how the CSV concept can be utilised by SMEs, a gap in Research that has been criticised for a long time (Karnani, 2007). As such the inductive approach is considered useful as it corresponds closely with the idea of this study to analyse observations, searching for patterns and formulating a theory towards the end of that process. The process is described as beginning with observation leading to empirical generalisations and a theory (Neumann, 2003, p. 51). *'Empirical research works by the process of induction'* (Goddard and Melville, 2004, p. 32).

Theories derived via inductive work may prove wrong, which is why theories should tested repeatedly. It is also important to understand that theories may not be universally valid. Thus it must be maintained that this study aims to establish a limited generalisation of the observations made which can be achieved by controlling the variables of the research. Repeated testing of such a theory then can increase confidence in its validity, given the condition that variables are reproduced to exclude the possibility of error of measurement (ibid, pp. 32-33). Furthermore this study can be suitable for an initial feasibility check before more resources are committed for further in-depth research.

The contextual change to which Porter's concept is applied and the constraints of this research require a different setup for conducting the research than previously used. Therefore the case study, used by previous research focussing on MNCs (Williams and Hayes, 2013) will not be utilised and instead owners of SMEs are interviewed to reach the aims of the research. The involvement in daily business activities (Nooteboom, 1993, p. 288) makes owners the ideal source of information vital to meet these aims.

3.2.1. Collection and Analysis of Qualitative Data

Often studies on CSV have focussed on quantified findings (Porter et al., 2012); a fact that has been criticized (ibid) yet not without highlighting the difficulty of gathering all qualitative aspects (ibid).

For this study semi structured interviews have been chosen as the main source of qualitative data. Quantitative data does not help understanding the actions of owners and SMEs nor would it answer the research questions. As stated above the lack of qualitative data, but also the focus this study has chosen makes qualitative data the desired information. Hence quantifications are not the data of choice given the fact that opinions and perceptions are the key items to be investigated. Qualitative data gathered via semi structured interviews will allow identification of patterns and thus enable interpretation of parameters that influence awareness of CSV but also the likeliness of successful implementation.

Semi structured interviews with the owners of SMEs will gather the information needed directly from the person most likely to be best informed about the company. While being deeply involved in daily operations (Nooteboom, 1993, p. 288), owners are argued to be the source of the information desired.

3.2.2. The Qualitative Approach

The data sought to reach the aim of the study is all qualitative in nature. It is concerned with perceptions and motivations, factors that have no quantities. Therefore appropriate data collection methods have been chosen, all part of qualitative research. SME business owners are considered the driving source of this research and as the research is concerned with the natural environment of the business, a qualitative approach is the method of choice (Bryman and Bell, 2003, p. 302,303).

An exact definition of qualitative research is still lacking (Bryman and Bell, 2003, p. 311) but it is acknowledged to be more open-ended than quantitative research. Theories and concepts are developed through and by the research process and thus are considered outcomes of the research (ibid) making qualitative approaches suitable for inductive studies. In summary a new dimension for the concept of CSV is more likely to be developed by qualitative approaches and interaction with the research subject.

The approach itself has received criticism of various sources. Quantitative researchers for example dispute the validity caused by the lack of solid evidence (facts and figures). Further criticism labels qualitative research as *'too subjective'* (Bryman and Bell, 2003, p. 299), and *'difficult to replicate'* (ibid, p. 300). It is argued that findings are problematic to generalise and many problems arise from a *'lack of transparency'* (ibid). The nature of qualitative research is not leading to ultimate truths, backed with solid facts and figures and was not established to do so.

However, there is also the argument that in an ever changing business world such generalisation is not possible (Saunders et al., 2007, p. 107). As a result qualitative research needs to be very specific concerning the determining criteria of its findings. It is acknowledged that findings of qualitative research are valid only for a certain set of criteria. The criteria have then been described and for the research sample also summarised in order to make them accessible and replicable.

Whereas the lack of transparency can be accommodated by detailed description of the research parameters, 'subjectivity' is hard if not impossible to eliminate (Barney et al., 2013) and may also be a part of the whole design (Saunders, 2009, fig. 4.2. p. 119).

The description of this research fits the philosophy of Interpretivism where values are important, subjective meanings (such as motivation of actions) and the details of the situation are vital for an understanding. Furthermore, it is argued that human beings interpret their surroundings but also their own actions (Onwuegbuzie, 2000). Thus social realities are constructed by actions and perceptions (Haralambos and Holborn, 2008, p. 793; Snyder and Swann Jr., 1978; Spinelli, 2005, p. 12) yet a full discussion of Interpretivism and modern hermeneutics would go beyond the purpose of this research.

3.2.3. Semi Structured Interviews

Semi structured interviewing is not limited to a fixed set of questions but allows the researcher to shape interview questions during interviewing, which is often directed by participants' responses. During an interview it is possible that certain information leads to expanding a topic and answers to questions can open completely new approaches and datasets for the researcher. Initially a number of topics or themes are targeted and depending upon participants' answers new ideas can develop that are investigated.

The semi structured interview is considered less intrusive to the interviewee (Bryman, 2001, pp. 319, 331; UN Food and Agricultural Organization, 1990). It does formulate a certain general topic that is to be investigated but other than guidance the interviewee and interviewer have an amount of freedom to act and interact during the interview. Therefore semi structured interviews are the method of choice when the views of the interviewee are important (Bryman and Bell, 2003, p. 365).

Such leeway could be criticised for lack of rigidity but the essential data that is sought for this study depends not only on such leeway but also on the cooperation of the interviewees. Emphasising on interaction and thus fostering a closer acquaintance between interviewer and interviewee they are perceived to make discussion of sensitive topics easier for both parties (UN Food and Agricultural Organization, 1990). In other words the interviewees may experience less distance towards the interviewer and closeness is argued to be a requirement in research on small firms (Shaw, 1999). With 'closeness' research participants may then more easily reveal their own opinion rather than consider first what answer might be most beneficial. Further will interaction allow a much broader and deeper view at the phenomenon that is being studied. Hence the criticism concerning lacking rigidity is not a flaw but deliberate choice.

The questions have been designed to determine owners' awareness of CSR and CSV and to give an insight how they perceive both concepts. The semi structured approach with open ended questions will produce the desired data concerning opinions and value judgements of SME owners. Further the concept is open to diversion in many directions in order to fully grasp owners' views and to follow the information flow where it leads to

3.2.4. Research Sample and Sampling Method

The study applied the convenience sampling method to select a sample of ten SMEs, each represented by their owner. In one case where the organisation has four owners they nominated one to be interviewed on behalf of the company. None of the SMEs' workforce size exceeds the number of four, which reflects statistical data in a number of publications (European Commission, 2005; Federation of Small businesses, 2013; US Census Bureau, 2008). Participants have been selected from both the UK (n = 8) as well as Germany (n = 2) and from a variety of sectors.

Convenience sampling can be used for any research and has certain advantages and disadvantages. Drawing on research participants that are easily available (Marshall, 1996) the method offers a convenient way of completing a time constrained data collection. However the availability also raises the question how representative such a sample could be (Babbie, 2013; Blaikie, 2009).

Firstly it should be understood that convenience sampling is more common than expected (Bryman and Bell, 2003) and due to constraints of this research more elaborate methods were unfeasible to employ. Secondly the criticism concerning sampling bias, particularly validity and the problems concerning generalisation, could be applied whenever the sample is smaller than the total population. On the other hand the highly individualistic nature of SMEs (Stoian et al., 2012) would result in a research sample that is partly random and findings therefore easier to apply in the SME context. The owners of the selected SMEs come from a variety of backgrounds, educational levels and business sectors. As stated before any sample and qualitative, inductive research is open to questions concerning validity to some extent.

Outlining the determining criteria of such a research will make the outcomes repeatable and therefore increase validity (Bryman and Bell, 2003, p. 300). It should also be noted that many interpretivists reject the goal of generalisation as such (Schofield, 2002, p. 173) and that any research *'must be seen as carrying its own logic, sense of order, structure and meaning'* (Denzin, 1983). This emphasises on the context of the research but further broadening of the topic would go beyond the aim of this study.

Further debate concerns the selection of different industry sectors and the fact that SMEs residing in two different countries are investigated. Previous studies on CSV have been conducted across a number of different business sectors (Klein, 2011; Porter and Kramer, 2011; Williams and Hayes, 2013), therefore the participants of this research also come from a variety of industries. The issue of different countries of origin seemingly is a larger one. It is acknowledged that there are differences between the UK and Germany concerning factors that could influence SMEs structure and development such as the legal framework. This could lead could to a different perception and implementation of CSV.

However it should first be noted that both countries also show significant similarities in the historic development of their industry and CSR policies. The founding of worker villages for example happened in both countries at the same stage of industrialisation (Grollmann, 1996; Smith, 2003; Vonde, 2012). Therefore it could also be argued that CSR and CSV do depend rather on perception and view than on legal framework. Both concepts are set on top of legal and business imperatives. Different national culture could lead to different ways of implementation but historically the case of the workers villages, as discussed in the literature review, disputes this. Therefore country of origin would probably have negligible impact on findings.

Finally the study aims to set the stage for future research rather than answer all questions concerning the concept of CSV in SMEs. It is therefore considered reasonable not to use industrial sectors or specific countries as sampling criteria.

3.3. Data Analysis

Data was audio recorded and transcribed. All data were collected completely anonymous and analysed to recognise patterns and communalities across the sets of data. The analysis is loosely based on the model offered by Shaw (1999) shown in figure 3.

Figure 3 'The process of inductive analyses'

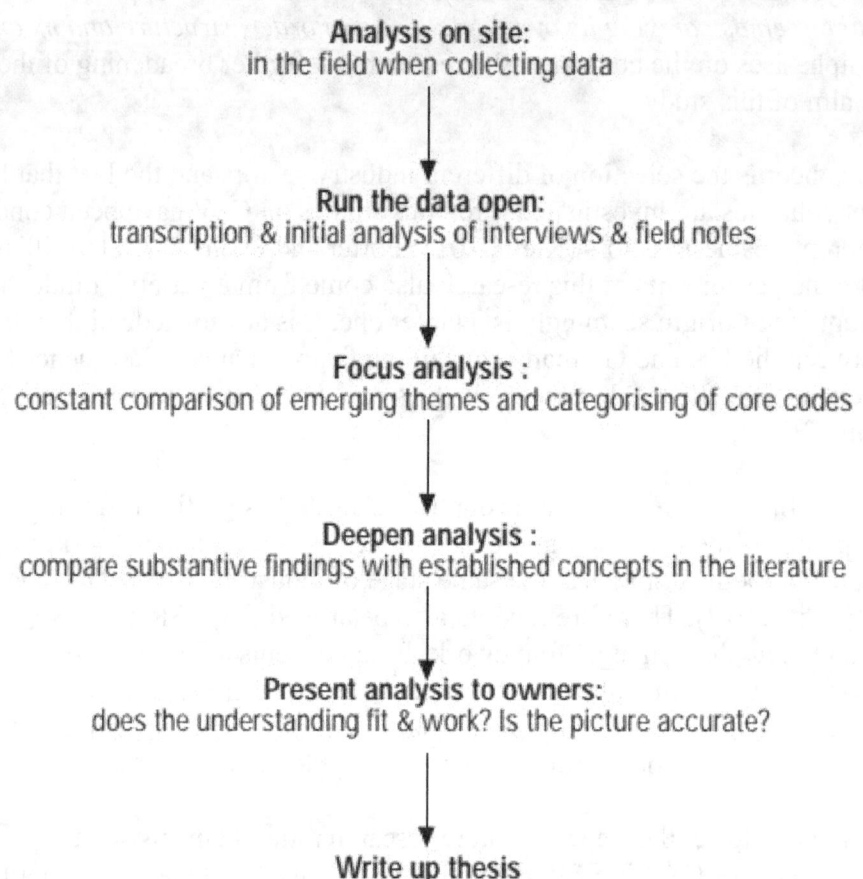

Source: Shaw (1999)

An initial analysis during the interview process was used to validate information and to probe further explanation where applicable. Interviewees' answers and reflections upon these guided the interview. During transcription further analysis of each interview was undertaken and served as a base to which consecutive interviews were compared. A deeper understanding was developed in an in depth analysis of the transcriptions and the audio files of the interviews. Word 2010 was used to identify and search for certain keywords and patterns to establish themes and topics that can answer the research questions.

To improve understanding the audio files have been replayed numerous times. Recorded voice has the advantage of conveying the atmosphere and tone of voice which any written transcription naturally lacks. Patterns and themes can thus be identified and verified but also the 'meaning' of how answers were worded is important (Silverman, 2001). To accommodate the fact that interviewees' answers are shaped by their personal experience the analysis is footed on 'narration' (Bryman and Bell, 2003, p. 440). Narration is considered important for understanding the individuality and reasoning of decisions as well as the 'story' of the business which is crucial in grasping the perception and implementation of CSV. It could also make the existence of certain obstacles and benefits more accessible.

3.4. Ethical considerations

As every research raises concerns among various groups it is understood that the researcher needs to be aware of ethical implications and adhere to a certain conduct. For this research all data is collected anonymously to protect individuals' rights. All participants are fully informed about the research and prior to the interview sign a consent form which explains their rights in detail. The sheet can be found as Appendix B. The ethical committee of Heriot Watt University has reviewed and approved the researcher's statements concerning the research. Certain behavioural patterns and acceptable conduct during research is vital and thus not an issue. The researcher is aware that adverse behaviour will have the most severe impact on quality and validity of the study.

3.5. Data Validity

Qualitative studies and convenience samples are criticised for limited validity (Babbie, 2013; Blaikie, 2009; Neumann, 2003; Patton, 2002; Shaw, 1999). Also such data often cannot be generalised. Therefore secondary sources such as companies' internet appearances and literature on SMEs and CSV were reviewed to verify and understand the patterns discovered during data analysis. Triangulating with secondary data therefore will make sense of findings and increase validity of the researcher's discoveries (Denzin, 1970; Silverman, 2001, p. 233). Particularly the literature mentioned in Section 2 was used to verify findings.

Respondent validation (Silverman, 2001, p. 233) was used during the interviews, summarising and paraphrasing what the interviewer understood, probing the interviewees to acknowledge, clarify and dispute leading to data that represents the interviewees' views as authentic as possible. Further questions concerning validity of data have been addressed throughout the methodology chapter.

3.6. Limitations of the Research and Addressing them

As an exploration of the subject the study is not without limitation and can raise debate in several ways. As an MSc dissertation there is limited time to complete the whole work. The concept of CSV is considered established within MNCs and it is acknowledged that SMEs have been studied solely on the receiving end of it (Williams and Hayes, 2013). Here the concept of CSV is studied whether SMEs could become creators rather than receivers and what benefits and difficulties are to be expected. As early as 2007 this gap in research had been identified and criticised (Karnani, 2007).

Questions could arise by using more than one language. Besides English the interviews have also been conducted with German organisations in their native language (German). The translation from German into English could lead to a loss of information, partly because of possibly poor command of the language(s) but mostly due to a bias of the translator. Meanings could be interpreted wrongly or lost in a translation due to such bias (Peña, 2007).

The researcher is also acting as translator and is a native speaker of both languages. Although all German participants have a sufficient command of English, interviews were held in German and translated thereafter. It is argued that respondent validation and the prior acquaintance of the researcher with the participants would lessen if not eliminate the issues.

The researcher piloted the designed methodology with the supervisor shaping it into the discussed version. Further improvements, particularly of the interview process were implemented during the process of research. Feedback and experience from previous interviews helped enhancing the quality of subsequent events.

In summary it is argued that the constraints of this research have little effect on its validity. As an exploration the main target is to look at the possibility of CSV being used by SMEs to create shared value, to assess what obstacles need to be overcome and what benefits could potentially be realised. A more in depth analysis particularly of the latter two would be a matter of future research.

3.7. Summary of Research Design

The research is designed as an exploratory study on the possibility of creating shared value by SMEs. Therefore a deliberate approach and design have been chosen to obtain an overview on the possibility of CSV being created by SMEs. The research itself is subject to continuous process improvement. The study will adhere to ethical standards. Validity of data has been discussed and limitations have been considered and addressed. The research does not intend to answer all questions concerning the topic but to lead to further research.

4. Findings and Discussion

4.1. Chapter Overview

This chapter provides discussion on findings. Three main themes are identified, awareness of CSR and CSV, motivation for (non-)implementation and the difficulties and benefits SMEs experience when engaging in the concepts.

While all participants were aware of CSR as such; their definitions of CSR were diverse. Financial and administrative difficulties were mentioned as main obstacles of feasibility slowing or hindering implementation of CSR or CSV. Among the reported benefits it is the owners' view to achieve an advantage over their competitors by realising better prices for their products.

This research is probably among early attempts to study CSV in SMEs. Whereas CSR in SMEs has been researched, with the conclusion that implementation is possible under certain circumstances, there is very limited study on CSV in this context. Data collection was slightly hampered as some owners limited their answers to certain questions. Consequently some businesses that were approached chose not to support this study, assuming what they do concerning CSR or CSV was not the right thing or not enough and could damage their reputation.

The remaining participants however offered rich data and cover a multitude of possible constellations. As mentioned in the methodology chapter owners are directly or indirectly revealing potentially sensitive information. It is the researcher's view that the relationship with research participants has led to adequate data and in-depth information.

4.2. Summary of Research Sample

The research sample consists of ten companies from both the UK (n=8) and Germany (n=2) covering a variety of possible constellations. These companies are between 1 and 20+ years old and their owners' age group ranges from the 20-30 to over 50. Educational background was also diverse from high school diploma to higher education. The owners had different motives for starting the business venture where some started their business as a hobby or due to the lack of their own interest being covered by another occupation. Others were looking for a career, desiring to be their own boss or wanted to work in a way their current employer would not accommodate. Also the amount of work experience varied from many years of being employed to lifelong entrepreneurs.

Data shows how diverse small businesses are and consequently the approach to CSR or CSV will be different for every business. Following the notion of Nooteboom (1993, p. 288), owners are a central figure and thus very influential in how the business operates. Themes identified during analysis and presented in the findings will be contextualised with literature on the topic of CSR and CSV. The discussion will start with the awareness of CSR and CSV where it is argued that the variety of definitions is neither surprising nor detrimental to the awareness as such. CSV on the other hand being widely unknown is leading to the proposal to integrate CSV back into CSR.

Owners' motivation for (not) implementing CSR or CSV is discussed briefly before the perceived difficulties and benefits are elaborated in more detail as understanding these difficulties and benefits is important. The research has given evidence that many owners are willing to engage in the topic but encounter many difficulties that need to be overcome. Financial and administrative shortcomings are the main reasons but also the varieties of CSR definitions are mentioned before the successful CSV examples of the study are highlighted. The role of policymakers is then focussed upon. Besides increasing attention and interest SMEs still do not perceive they are receiving the support they would need.

Finally the experienced and potential benefits are elaborated. These include the possibility to 'use' CSR or CSV to gain an advantage over other competitors, regardless of their size. Moreover it is argued that smaller businesses could be more flexible and respond faster to the requirements of the marketplace – which could be advantageous to implement new agendas.

Figure 4: Overview of Research Sample

Name of Company	Country of Registration	Age of Company (years)	Agegroup of owner(s)	Educational level of owner(s)*	Number of employees (owners)	Awareness of CSR**	CSR is used***	Awareness of CSV**	CSV is used***
Company A	UK	2	50+	2	0 (1)	Y	++	N	+
Company B	GER	16	40+	2	0 (1)	Y	++	N	+
Company C	UK	1	30+	3	2 (1)	Y	--	N	--
Company D	UK	4	30+	1	0 (1)	Y	o	N	o
Company E	GER	3+	30+	2	0 (1)	Y	++	N	n/a
Company F	UK	1	20+	3	0 (4)	Y	++	N	+
Company G	UK	7+	30+	3	0 (1)	Y	++	N	o
Company H	UK	2	40+	3	0 (3)	Y	o	N	o
Company I	UK	3	30+	2	2 (1)	Y	++	N	o
Company K	UK	20+	50+	2	n/a	Y	++	N	o

Key: GER = Germany
       UK = United Kingdom

* The educational level has been split into the following parts
   1 = Secondary school only
   2 = Secondary school and vocational training and/or college
   3 = Higher education (Bachelor and Master studies, or equivalent)

** Y = Yes, N = No

*** -- = CSR/CSV is deliberately not used, - = CSR/CSV is not used, o = CSR/CSV not used but owner would be interested, + = CSR/CSV is unconciously used, ++ = CSR/CSV is used deliberately, n/a = no information available

4.3. Finding 1: Awareness and Perception of CSR and CSV

All research participants had an idea of CSR, although definitions were highly individual. Where some owners emphasised on the fair treatment of their own workforce

> *"happy employees produce better results"* (Owner E)

other owners were very conscious of how their suppliers conduct business and yet others argued that a business should consider *'what is right'* (Owners A, B, D, G). A sense of justice could be argued to exist although not all decisions to do something good were entirely without self-interest. Treating employees in a particular way to achieve better results certainly also benefits the owner who is paying closer attention to the wellbeing of employees.

However one organisation was in dispute of CSR being a matter for businesses at all. It was argued that a business should focus on making money and leave any CSR to organisations which are particularly established for that purpose. Charities were considered as better vehicles for delivery of any CSR. The argument brought forward is that owners are generally interested in making money and CSR could interfere with that strife whereas a charity is established for the purpose of doing something good.

> *'Companies exist to make money, not for charitywork.'* (Owner C)

Prior to the interviews no organisation was aware of the concept of CSV and none of them distinguished between the two concepts. The notion that CSV implements CSR with the intention to make money caused interest in all but one organisation. Some organisations then questioned whether their approach to business and CSR was not in fact CSV.

> *'Taking these examples I wonder if that is not CSV as well'* (Owner A)

The idea of CSV was acknowledged as a near ideal solution for creating something good while still making money. It was argued to make implementation easier when the actions not only deliver benefits to stakeholders but also profits for the business. Potentially it should enable smaller companies with limited resources such as time and finance to engage in the concept more easily and as a result motivate more businesses to do the same.

'Of course it would be ideal for all sides if you can do both' – (Owner D)

Although a business approach is taken to create something good, all participants denied that doing good is fully devalued by the intention to make money. It was argued the outcome is still something good being created and even with the financial focus such a deed is important. However, the interviewees also showed a tendency to question the true intentions of large corporations. When investigated further it was discovered that there is limited trust in the honesty of MNCs. Prominent failures to live up to societal expectations apparently has created suspicion.

"They are too big. Who holds them responsible? How can they be trusted, when at the same time they abuse that trust?" (Owner A)

4.3.1. Awareness and Implementation Criteria - Owners as Decisive Factor

Although definition of CSR varied significantly, small businesses are generally aware of the concept and relating it to responsibilities towards society. CSV was agreed to offer the benefit of making money, which should make it easier for SMEs to 'buy in' and implement corresponding policies. With a multitude of definitions among academia already there is little surprise that SMEs approach to CSR policies is diverse and individual as highlighted in the literature review chapter.

This also confirms that awareness of and approach to CSR and CSV is depending on owners experience, values and perceptions. Formal education cannot serve as criteria when the validity of the concept is disputed by a business owner with a high level of education but embraced by an owner at the other end of the education spectrum. Said dispute however, is not uncommon and has been voiced previously (Friedman, 1972; Levitt, 1958). On the other hand it could be argued that owners perception and values are formed by their experience and type of education in general.

This would put attention to the philosophical and moral side of learning. Philosophical stance has also been quoted as a decision factor for actually implementing CSR and CSV policies by the research participants.

'Philosophy? Perhaps. I call it culture. It is up to each of us and personally I cannot even think of behaving otherwise.' (Owner B)

Therefore not the level but the composition of education could not only explain the varying degree of awareness of CSR and CSV but also the particular emphasis any approach of the concepts may take. In consequence there could be many equally valid forms of CSR and CSV coexistent and companies should choose the approach best suited their individual situation.

Lack of CSV awareness could have many reasons. Firstly the concept was first introduced in 2006 whereas original CSR dates back to the rise of organisations during the industrial revolution (Gjolberg, 2009). Secondly the majority of research has been focussed on CSR while CSV has been investigated solely on the basis of case studies and MNCs.

Thirdly the aforementioned multitude of valid definitions of CSR leaves room to consider CSV as one particular form of CSR. Similarities between Porter (2006, 2011) and Bhattacharya (2011) suggest that although initial intentions and focus were reportedly different, the outcomes in all cases were beneficial for all parties involved.

Whereas it is agreed that the CSV focus on making money while doing something good could make buy in and implementation easier as well as more feasible, the attitude of customers must be taken into account. It was argued that American customers focus more on the fact that something good is done whereas European customers are sceptical about business driven approaches (Bhattacharya and Sen, 2004). Customers may be reluctant to accept organisations involvement and question their intentions.

Success then becomes a matter of trust. Large corporate scandals were named as a main reason why trust in MNCs is limited, although it was acknowledged that some of them are doing good things. The sheer size of such organisations is regarded to be a problem, leaving the problem for society whom to hold accountable and how (see Quote from Owner A, p. 39). Smaller organisations are perceived to be much more transparent on this matter. Literature acknowledges SMEs to have closer relations to stakeholders and being deeply rooted in the local communities. Thus, trust in the organisation is identical with trusting the owner. An owner can create such trust by being reliable and consistent. Authenticity and walking the talk are essential, failure to live up to self-set standards will ultimately result in mistrust.

As a result, interest, implementation and success depend to varying extent on the owner as a central figure. To increase awareness and implementation it is the owners that need to be informed and their perceptions altered. The role of policymakers in this matter will be discussed in a separate section.

4.4. Finding 2: Motivation for (Non-)implementation

Among interviewed owners there are three general opinions towards CSR and CSV and the feasibility for the business to implement it. Firstly the concept is disputed completely, secondly it is considered interesting if it can also make money and thirdly it is at the core of the business and the business itself designed around it.

One of the participants completely denies any responsibility of the business concerning CSR/CSV. Whereas the concept is not disputed per se, it is argued that a business is run to make money and other issues should not interfere with this. It is agreed that certain behavioural patterns are to be expected and the legal framework to be followed. Yet further responsibility is denied and highlighted that organisations like charities are set up for these purposes.

> *'You would not sell products to people when you doubt their intentions.'* (Owner C)

The majority of organisations are not only advocating responsibilities of the business and its owner, they are also interested in how they could fulfil these obligations. The concern raised is how a business should conduct operations responsibly when their owner is tied up in daily operations and the small business entities are financially not affluent enough beyond making a living for their owner. It is also argued that governmental influence and encouragement is lacking in this particular area. Businesses are looking for guidance and assistance on how to implement CSR and how they could fulfil their obligations, but support and opportunities are generally not present except where the businesses organise these among themselves like in the third group which is discussed below.

> *'At the end of the day you want to make money, fair enough. But what good can you do when you are a small business? The best most of us can do is donate to charity. They are in THAT business, they know, we don't.'* (Owner D)

> *'Most companies recognise these obligations. But the best they can do from their position is support charities or local projects. On a larger scale we have no voice.'* (Owner E).

Only two participants appeared to actively follow CSR policies and both were found to create shared value to some extent. A more detailed discussion why these are perceived to have implemented CSV follows in the section 4.5.4. 'Successful CSV'.

These owners are found to hold very specific opinions on CSR, believing certain values and behaviour should be applied as a businessman. Also these owners highlight multiple responsibilities of the business towards society. It is argued that the business does not stand by itself. On the contrary it is a part of society and its success depends on how well it is connected and engaged with it.

'As a business but also as a human being I am responsible not to screw up the planet for future generations. People are realising that, customers start being very conscious and question what you are doing and what not.' (Owner B)

Interaction with society and being considered an integral part of it is perceived to be vital for the survival of the business. Consequently these owners attempt to deliver their value proposition in a way they believe to be beneficial for society and also accept and fulfil wider expectations. Even more, it occurred to one owner that his actions were fulfilling a need that society had, back when he started offering it, not yet defined as being existent. In this case the owner is making space available where young people can meet and play but also learn a variety of skills. The owner believes these opportunities to create a positive influence for young people to pick up skills and *'do something different than getting drunk and being a nuisance to the public'* (Owner B).

Furthermore both owners were clear that repeatedly failing to meet societal expectations would detach the business from its surrounding and logically lead to its own failure when customers refuse to interact with them and do their business elsewhere. Making society better is considered important and a duty of everybody. Both owners concur that this desire is deeply rooted in them and quoted 'values' and 'philosophy' as the main argument for their opinions.

"It is a way of life. My conscience tells me to act this way, I cannot help it but follow it. It is what I think is right." (Owner A).

While the majority of participants were keen to engage in CSR more, they also highlighted a number of constraints that hinder their efforts. It was argued that lack of time and money but also absence of guidance and support were the main reasons why few smaller organisations implement CSR policies. Success of these policies could be increased if said obstacles could be accommodated for and overcome.

4.4.1. Philosophy, education or culture

The individuality of CSR and CSV implementation partly comes from different perceptions of the respective business owners. Most of the research participants voiced strong opinions for their particular interpretation of CSR. As stated above they perceive themselves to fulfil a certain duty towards society that is compliant with their own views of morality.

The motivation itself is impossible to be fixed on one criterion. Nonetheless the terms 'ethics', 'philosophy' and 'culture' were named as reasons why the owners engaged in the particular CSR or CSV activities. Education can only serve as an explanation to a limited extent. It appears that the surrounding, the society and its culture were influential on the owners and in turn also towards the particular route of CSR and CSV.

4.5. Finding 3: Difficulties, Benefits and Successes

Implementation of CSR and CSV policies was not a smooth and straightforward process for both companies that successfully utilized the concept. Also the businesses that are interested in doing 'more' voiced their concerns over potential difficulties but generally acknowledged the benefits that could possibly be achieved.

First and foremost all companies are in agreement that the financial situation of most SMEs does not allow the business to project large investments with only long term and indirect returns. While many small businesses do recognise the validity and necessity of companies giving something back to society they are facing a situation where they are struggling to meet legal requirements. The competitive environment leaves small businesses 'fighting to survive', owners are tied up complying with regulations and have no money or time to go beyond what is mandated by the legal framework.

> *'How? You work the whole day to make money and comply with all rules imposed on you. There is no time and money for extras.'* – (Owners C, D)

Furthermore owners were in agreement that one small business cannot make a difference besides honestly trying.

> *'I do not think my supplier really cares other than having yet another niche seller in the UK'* (Owner A)

> *'As a business partner I am too small to tell my supplier what to do.*
> *Luckily I found a supplier that has the same philosophy as I do*
> *so I can do business with him the way I want to.*
> *Other relationships are more or less*
> *'take it or leave it' '* (Owner B)

It is suggested that a greater amount of coordination could give small businesses the voice they need in order to be heard and to combine efforts in order to create an impact similar to that of a large MNC engaging in these concepts. Coordination and guidance are also agreed to compensate for the lack of knowledge a single business entity can have. Owners are unsure if their approach would be regarded as correct and whether their efforts are enough.

> *'Oh is it? I thought it was just normal business'* (Owner B)

Overcoming these difficulties is crucial not only to increase the possibility of success or feasibility but could also lead to greater awareness of CSR and CSV as well as the potential benefits by increasing the number of success stories. Concerning benefits it is experienced that customers do value the responsibility of the owners and their businesses. While doing something good is appreciated, it is also emphasised that doing good must be trustworthy. Hence the owner must be trustworthy, which is perceived to be achievable by being consistent and authentic. Failing to meet the values communicated to the public on the other hand is argued to be a direct route to business failure. If the business partner cannot be believed, customers would be likely to go elsewhere.

It is confirmed by all businesses that customers not only value such approach but also are willing to pay a premium for products matching certain ethical criteria. Thus potentially higher prices sourcing these products are offset by customers' willingness to pay higher prices as well. All owners agreed that there is a limit to customers' acceptance of higher prices but were unable to quantify such limit. The closest idea they offered was 'being reasonable'.

Owners A and B who successfully utilised their social responsibility also mentioned the benefit of increased cooperation with other businesses, particularly suppliers. Although formal coordination is lacking, a closer relationship among businesses and working together on certain projects is considered beneficial for all parties involved. One owner gave an example of a large supplier appreciating feedback given concerning the order process and worked with several smaller buyers to improve that process, saving all parties time and also money.

> *'They realised even my small business has some good ideas
> and if they take feedback in this way they can improve their own processes.
> More suppliers should cooperate like this'* (Owner B)

This mandates mutual interest not only to exist but also that both sides meet at the same level. Cooperation, especially where one partner has a dominant position was said to be rather the exception than the case.

As stated in the above section concerning motivation it is again emphasised that every little step is perceived to make society better. Essentially the values and perceptions of the owners were instrumental towards their approach to CSR. In consequence they also applied these values and perceptions and at least partly used them for making business decisions.

4.5.1. Financial and organisational constraints

As literature suggested, owners are heavily involved in daily operations of the business. When concerned with general scarcity of finance CSR and CSV stand a higher chance of success when they are closely related to daily business and require little financial effort. Therefore CSV should be the preferred option for SMEs as it is not only a business activity but also generates revenue in the process.

While CSV would accommodate both financial and time constraints, SMEs question whether or not their small size can create enough impact to make a difference. It is understood that an SME cannot reach the footprint as a larger organisation would. It is argued that giving SMEs a bigger voice could result in their CSR implementation being more widely known and having a larger impact.

In respect to daily customer contact, impact is created mostly via word of mouth. With finance being constraint SMEs cannot afford advertisement to the extent larger businesses can. Recent research suggests underdeveloped marketing channels such as Social Media (Bulearca and Bulearca, 2010; Woodcock et al., 2011) could offer SMEs a larger footprint without decreasing already scarce finance. How SMEs could start utilising social media uncovered another theme where difficulties need to be overcome and structures developed if SMEs are supposed to increase engagement and impact in CSR/CSV. Existing structures seem to be inefficient to increase and encourage CSR or CSV activities and therefore fail to utilise the business potential of SMEs.

4.5.2. Guidance and Support – The Role of Policymakers

The general response of interviewees suggests policymakers were not supportive of smaller companies in general. Particularly concerning CSR or CSV implementation it is argued that there is little to no support for SMEs. Besides lack of finance and time, this was named as one of the reasons why the owners did not follow up their ideas for implementing a social component into their business. All initiative was reported to come from the business owners themselves without outside assistance. Policymakers' interest is considered to be put almost exclusively on large corporations while small businesses are left on their own.

Nonetheless policymakers are showing increasing support for SMEs, be it in legislation offering SMEs certain benefits over larger businesses, e.g. in taxation; or increasing interest documented in a number of EU papers and clear acknowledgements of SMEs as highly important drivers of the economy. In daily practice not much of these are experienced by SME owners and neither is the increasing interest of academia in SMEs. It seems clear it should be the majority of the economy that is taken into consideration in order to understand and manage it.

The perception of business owners therefore suggests that there is a gap in communication from policymakers and information does not reach the intended recipients. One reason could be the aforementioned lack of time owners have due to business operations and thus a new and more direct way to communicate needs to be established to increase the amount of support that actually reaches the target. Increasing communication could be done utilising existing structures and bodies such as the chamber of commerce. These communication channels would need to be used frequently in order to attract and retain SME owners.

The first question all participants had during interviews was concerning how they should fulfil their duties towards society and how exactly these duties were defined. Besides the various definitions of CSR (Dahlsrud, 2008) it also shows the long negligence of SMEs from researchers, interest groups and policymakers. Relevant research has picked up since Castka (2004) and policymakers have also begun realising the importance of SMEs culminating in a multitude of papers by the European Union focussing on SMEs. Yet this is seemingly not enough.

Owners called for accessible information made available locally. Local councils and small business advocacy groups are called upon to assist owners with these ideas and help them implement them. A thriving local business community should be in the best interest of the economy as a whole. It is alarming that no owner was aware of any of the papers by the European Commission, nor could any representative be named that could be approached for guidance and support concerning CSR topics. Not surprisingly ISO 26000 as a draft for CSR Standards is unknown as well. Initiatives such as the successful examples in this research have been undertaken solely by the owners of the respective businesses and their business partners.

In summary the advances that have been made by research and policymakers need to be more focussed. Local interest and advocacy groups could offer their representation to give SMEs a larger voice and in return receive the support and guidance these companies are looking for. Good ideas are available but the execution is improvable. Therefore SMEs would be well-advised to organise their CSR efforts better. One possible option would call for the local chamber of industry and commerce to take up the role as an advisor. Not only would this solve the issue of guidance and support but also possibly bring coordination to a very diverse approach to CSR.

Another benefit could be realised if such a coordinator serves as a matchmaker bringing businesses with similar ideas together so they can help one another. Furthermore an organisation representing multiple SMEs is harder to ignore or pass by than a single SME. Large corporations might be more interested to talk to such a representative than to a single owner run shop.

A coordinated approach, uniting many SMEs under one entity would then also increase the impact. With impact increasing more SMEs could then be interested in these activities and further enlarge success.

4.5.3. Confusing versions of CSR and CSV – Uniting definitions

The hesitation of businesses to engage in CSR or CSV and the doubts concerning such engagement is only partly due to the lack of guidance and support. The abundance of CSR definitions and the introduction of CSV as a new concept seemingly not improve the situation. Owners often abandon their ideas because lack of finance or time but also because of the difficulties of finding a definition that fits and suits the situation of the business in question.

At the same time owners constantly underestimate the impact they can achieve by implementing a CSR or CSV policy. Again, the multitude of definitions and the perceived lack of one definition that is suitable for the given business and situation diminishes the position an SME and in summary the whole group could potentially have.

Therefore a flexibility of approach is called for. An approach that can be tailored around the particular situation the business is experiencing. In respect to CSV the definition given by Porter (2011) should be broadened and incorporated with the suggestion of Bhattacharya (2011) to form an understanding that CSV can be achieved by uniting business imperatives and responsible interaction with society. Thus CSV would be achieved whenever a business finds the opportunity to create revenue and at the same time gives something back to society. The possibility to do so and potential benefits have been described in many publications.

Furthermore the dissemination of CSR and CSV could be criticised. As Porter (1991) argues a dissemination of the business into 'core competencies' removes the bigger picture of the organisation and thus the understanding of it is seriously diminished. Not only does this argue for a holistic view of the business but consequently a more holistic view on CSR and CSV. Any CSR or CSV in the business then cannot be separated from the business, its processes and structures. On the contrary would CSR and CSV then become integral part of the business and cannot be disseminated from it. Consequently processes and structures will evolve more natural as opposed to organisations that add CSR or CSV on top of their business model for any given reason. Such organisations could have difficulty to integrate an out of place item – no matter how flexible and fitting its definition may be. However, a broader definition and holistic understanding of CSR and CSV alone will not suffice.

As stated before an independent body to govern and manage many SMEs CSR activities could solve the problems of coordination, guidance and support while also creating momentum to unite more SMEs under one banner. Yet the starting point should be a very general definition of CSR and also include CSV. As absolute definitions would have contrary effects. Paired with that central point of information, SMEs could then coordinate their different approaches and being represented by an organisation that speaks for many SMEs with one voice will achieve the impact that is necessary.

Besides the absence of ideal ground to start from there are small businesses that have successfully implemented CSR or CSV. In the research sample Company A and B were identified being successful to some extent. In both cases the owners had very clear expectations from their ventures, deeply rooted ethical values and the determination to make their approach a success.

4.5.4. Successful CSV

With evidence of two companies successfully creating shared value, it could be stated that successful implementation of CSV, much like that of CSR, depends on a number of circumstances and criteria (Baden et al., 2009; Castka et al., 2004; Forum Europe, 2012). Flexibility of approach could accommodate for the differences of MNCs and SMEs, giving SMEs the opportunity to engage in a form of CSR that is tailor-made for them, namely CSV.

In both present cases the owners had a very clear vision what they wanted to achieve with 'business' being a central motivation. The design in both cases is also heavily influenced by the strong ethical and moral perceptions of the owners. Both owners reported the lack of support and guidance and highlighted the route to achieve success was drawn not only by them but also their business partners who cooperated with them.

These partnerships replaced formal assistance and guidance whereas coordination was achieved by direct communication of all involved parties. Thus a joint vision was shaped and implemented. Interaction with one another, designing supply chains and products did in those cases not end the actions. In both cases these links were extended when suppliers in return improved their policies as well. Shared value was created and in the following section some of the benefits experienced are presented.

4.5.5. Benefits of Implementation

While implementation of CSR or CSV needs to overcome a number of difficulties it can also realise a number of benefits. If an organisation can get around the constraints mentioned above, their actions could lead to positive experiences like two SMEs of this study reported. These include achieving competitive advantage via better prices and reputation, increased cooperation with other businesses allowing the sharing of ideas and experiences and in return more successful approaches to social responsibility as well as financial advantages thorough better Supply Chain Management. Although impact is considered limited it should also be noted that the impact and benefits affect directly and solely the involved organisations. 'Outsiders' cannot profiteer from these efforts. Thus a bandwagon effect could be argued to exist, motivating spectators to become activists.

The perceived willingness of customers to pay higher prices for goods that match certain criteria could be only a relative advantage as the sourcing price possibly is also be higher than with products that do not match these criteria, most importantly though these criteria are set and monitored by the vendor but whether the products really match these criteria and moreover if the set of criteria is the desired one is entirely up to the customer. The sense for a good business opportunity is not changing just because some sort of CSR is being involved. In consequence an ethical product is not coming to life if it is not marketable.

Also this focuses attention on customer satisfaction as still being the key to continued business success. 'Happy customers are the best marketing'. Customer loyalty will in turn increase business success via a product that matches or exceeds customer expectations and at the same time fills a niche by complying with certain ethical criteria. Satisfying customer desire in an ethically good manner will then increase reputation, as long as the business itself is perceived as trustworthy. The importance of trust has been discussed before.

As product design and selection of criteria is important, cooperation with potential suppliers can benefit both businesses and in last consequence also the customer. If both suppliers and vendors engage in a cooperative manner to design a product, minimise wastage and manage to optimise production they can leverage financial benefits by lowering cost of production and supply. Another attempt to lower cost could be to localise production of goods. In itself a potentially ethical criterion ('local produce') it opens the room for fresher goods, produced upon need and with a lower impact on the environment as transportation to the customer is faster and quicker compared to centralised production, the downside being the possible lack of scale economies.

Introducing high quality, ethically correct products a small business can distinguish itself from its competitors and gain competitive advantage over them. Decisive here would be whether consumers value the different approach and whether the goods are of adequate quality. These factors, however, also apply for any other business decision and any company whether they engage in social responsibility or not. Both participants that implemented a form of CSV also argued that such notion must come based on owners' values and the business processes must be designed with a social awareness in mind. Calling for a holistic approach both owners unknowingly solved their problem how to be authentic when attempting CSR.

'...holistic approach...not additionally...from the start' - (Owner G)

Customers are aware when a business is designed with such notion as opposed to companies that attempt to implement CSR 'on top' of existing processes and structures, the latter being more likely to fail. CSR remains an additional duty, whereas companies that design their processes considering CSR at every stage can grow 'naturally' into their position. Also owners that live CSR every day are more credible than those who add CSR to the agenda without really being convinced themselves. As stated before credibility and authenticity are the key variables for trust (Brown, 2012; Du et al., 2011).

The real advantage of SMEs would come to bear in the actual execution of business visions. While SMEs tend to have smaller and flatter hierarchies than MNCs (Supyuenyong et al., 2009) they are more flexible to react to the marketplace. In other words the SME owner having a business idea will get in touch with potential suppliers, design a product and start selling it whereas in MNCs such a business idea will need to go through a multitude of hierarchy levels before an implementation is made. Thus SMEs can easily achieve first mover advantage once they decide to move. Introducing a superior product faster than others, ever more so if it can be marketed as produced locally, would gain the seller an advantage over competitors that cannot make the same offer to the potential customers. Here again it must be stated that at the moment this potential is diminished without proper structures, so in order to achieve a wider success it will be inevitable to establish more formal structures, moving to less intuitive and individual approaches (European Commission, 2013b).

All efforts, however fail to impact if there are no attempts to commercialise them. As stated above small businesses do not have the ability to use mainstream media channels for advertising. Social media is an underdeveloped but interesting way to reach a broader audience (Bulearca and Bulearca, 2010; Woodcock et al., 2011). Both owners operate a business website and use social media to some extent but only one (Owner A) uses it to communicate the ethical component of their business. All other research participants do not use their homepage for other than pure business purposes.

4.6. Summary of Findings

In summary it is identified that CSV is indeed possible to implement in SMEs. Much like previous research on CSR in SMEs (Castka et al., 2004; Henshaw, 2011; Santos, 2011), where success depends on the circumstances of the SME and the way how CSR is implemented. It is argued that CSV needs the same approach. A more open definition of CSV, possibly re-integrating it in CSR, and improved structures are perceived to be the key criteria for successful CSR/CSV and for a wider application of these concepts. In the following chapter conclusions are drawn and some recommendations given how more SMEs could be interested in implementing CSR/CSV.

5. Conclusions and Suggestions

5.1. Overview

The research offers evidence that SMEs can, under certain circumstances, not only implement CSR bus also CSV. Not size but intention matters. There are numerous challenges that are not easy to overcome. It is argued that SMEs in particular would need some form of assistance and CSR and CSV would benefit from more formal structures being fully utilised or put into place.

In respect to the aims of the research and the research questions it can be stated that firstly SMEs are able to utilise the concept of CSV but the approach needs to match the organisation.

Secondly due to financial constraints and lack of time a number of difficulties need to be accommodated. Current structures appear to be ineffective of targeting SMEs or altering owners' perceptions. While owners are willing to commit themselves they experience a lack of support. If CSV is successfully implemented it is likely to create competitive advantage via a number of benefits such as customer loyalty and cooperation with other companies (Du et al., 2011; Goosen, 2009).

Thirdly where structures are inadequate successful implementation rests solely with the owner's determination. Improving success rates could be achieved if the business potential of small businesses is recognised and structures are made fit for purpose.

Finally awareness of CSR in SMEs is near 100%, the possibility to utilise it in the form of CSV was unknown prior to the research but participants generally embraced the idea of combining business imperatives with societal duties.

5.2. Conclusions

SMEs are well aware of CSR but many do not attempt to engage in it because of several obstacles such as absence of guidance and support but also from the perception that their potential impact is non-existent. Key to wider recognition, acceptance and usage of the concept should start with a more open definition of CSR and also a central point of support, guidance and assistance. Establishing a better coordination, perhaps via organisations like the chamber of commerce could solve many of these problems and in turn motivate more SMEs to implement CSR or CSV policies and projects.

Owners' motivation and philosophical views are crucial not only to make an SME attempt to engage in CSR and CSV concepts but also for potential success of such attempts. It also highlights the decisive role the owner attains in a small business. All activities are decided and designed by the owner. Hence successful CSR and CSV need committed owners. Their efforts could serve as a counterbalance to a narrow interpretation of capitalism and profit focus. Porter and Kramer (2011) suggest some profits to be more ethically valuable than others. In order to increase the number of organisations creating such profits, owners' perceptions need to be addressed. Again a coordinated effort and highlighting successful examples could motivate hesitating owners to commit themselves.

The concept of CSV seems unknown to SMEs but its potential is recognised. Uniting several definitions of CSR and the notion that CSR can be utilised for business success could merge both CSR and CSV into a single concept to achieve wider recognition. Realising that doing 'good' can be profitable (Castka et al., 2004; Du et al., 2010; Durmaz et al., 2011; Goosen, 2009) more organisations should then decide to implement the concept into their business. Successful implementation offers SMEs a variety of benefits.

Where CSR agendas have naturally grown into the business and its structures, it is an integral part of the organisation. Customers value the responsible actions of a business and are willing to reward the business by paying higher prices and doing repeated business (Bhattacharya and Sen, 2004; Du et al., 2010). Key to this success is trust customers gain in the business and its owner. Credibility is easier to achieve for SMEs but also hard to maintain. If trust can be maintained, an organisation can achieve competitive advantage over its competitors. This includes not only other locally competing SMEs but also local representations of large companies.

5.3. Suggestions and Recommendations

This last section of this work proposes a number of recommendations and suggestions for future research. This research has identified that successful implementation of CSV is possible at SME level and can achieve many benefits for the SME, its suppliers and customers.

To overcome the difficulties encountered by SMEs it is recommended to coordinate SMEs efforts and offer a central point of assistance, guidance and support. As stated above such an approach could unite multiple SMEs and let them speak with one voice and thus multiply their impact. Existing structures appear to be insufficient to transfer the message from its origin to its target.

These structures must then be utilised and where necessary improved to be fit for purpose. Also the different approaches to CSR and the concept of CSV must be communicated not as separate concepts but as one idea of how businesses can live up to their perceived responsibilities while leveraging these efforts into business success.

Additionally the awareness of success stories should be communicated more widely. The use of social media and also the communication via a central organisation would increase awareness among SMEs, other businesses but also the general public.

Future research is recommended to analyse successful CSV implementation in SMEs more closely as it has been possible at this scale. Particularly the experienced benefits, the impact of arguably inadequate structures and the question how SMEs could market their efforts more effectively deserve a closer investigation.

Whether companies engage in CSR to make money or because they deem it the right thing to do is of secondary matter. It is perceived that a wider application of CSR would lead to a better society. CSV as one way to implement CSR could, as Porter and Kramer (2011) suggest, make CSR more accessible and benefit both society and the business.

6. Reference

Babbie, E.R., 2013. The Practice of social research, 13th ed. Wadsworth Pulishing Co Inc, Belmont, CA.

Baden, D.A., Harwood, I.A., Woodward, D.G., 2009. The effect of buyer pressure on suppliers in SMEs to demonstrate CSR practices: An added incentive or counter productive? European Management Journal 27, 429–441. doi:10.1016/j.emj.2008.10.004

Barney, A., Choi, S., Clarke, C., Davis, H., Fill, K., Gobbi, M., Halnan, A., Maier, P., Moloney, J., Morris, D., Price, J., Smith, H., Swabey, C., Treves, R., Warner, J., Warren, A., Williams, I., 2013. Theme 7: Bias [WWW Document]. eResearch methods. URL http://www.erm.ecs.soton.ac.uk/theme7/bias.html (accessed 7.6.13).

Basefsky, S., Sweeney, S., 2006. Employment Relations in SMEs: The United States.

BBC, 2013. BBC News - Apple "among largest tax avoiders in US" - Senate committee [WWW Document]. BBC News. URL http://www.bbc.co.uk/news/business-22600984 (accessed 5.27.13).

Beck, T., Demirguc-Kunt, A., 2006. Small and medium-size enterprises: Access to finance as a growth constraint. Journal of Banking & Finance 30, 2931–2943. doi:10.1016/j.jbankfin.2006.05.009

Bhattacharya, C.B., 2011. Leveraging corporate responsibility: the stakeholder route to maximizing business and social value. Cambridge University Press, Cambridge ; New York.

Bhattacharya, C.B., Sen, S., 2004. Doing Better at Doing Good: WHEN, WHY, AND HOW CONSUMERS RESPOND TO CORPORATE SOCIAL INITIATIVES. California Management Review 47, 9–24.

Blaikie, N.W.H., 2009. Designing social research: the logic of anticipation, 2nd ed. ed. Polity Press, Cambridge, UK ; Malden, MA.

BMWi, 2012. BMWi - Publikationen [WWW Document]. BMWi. URL http://www.bmwi.de/DE/Mediathek/publikationen,did=506316.html (accessed 6.1.13).

Boutilier, R.G., Thomson, I., Consultants, O.C.G., 2011. Modelling and measuring the social license to operate: fruits of a dialogue between theory and practice, in: Social Licence to Operate Symposium, University of Queensland.

Brech, J., 1995. Shell - der Ölmulti in den Wochen danach - Nachrichten DIE WELT - DIE WELT [WWW Document]. Die Welt. URL http://www.welt.de/print-welt/article660351/Shell-der-Oelmulti-in-den-Wochen-danach.html (accessed 2.16.13).

Brown, S.M., 2012. Want Credibility? Be Consistent. [WWW Document]. Lead Change Group. URL http://leadchangegroup.com/want-credibility-be-consistent/ (accessed 2.7.13).

Bryman, A., 2001. Social research methods. Oxford University Press, Oxford ; New York.

Bryman, A., Bell, E., 2003. Business research methods. Oxford University Press, Oxford ; New York.

Bulearca, M., Bulearca, S., 2010. Twitter: a viable marketing tool for SMEs. Global Business and Management Research: An International Journal 2, 296–309.

Carroll, A.B., 1999. Corporate Social Responsibility: Evolution of a Definitional Construct. Business & Society 38, 268–295. doi:10.1177/000765039903800303

Carroll, A.B., 1991. The Pyramid of Corporate Social Responsibility: Toward the Moral Management of Organizational Stakeholders. Business Horizons 34, 39–48.

Carroll, A.B., Shabana, K.M., 2010. The Business Case for Corporate Social Responsibility: A Review of Concepts, Research and Practice. International Journal of Management Reviews 12, 85–105. doi:10.1111/j.1468-2370.2009.00275.x

Castka, P., Balzarova, M.A., Bamber, C.J., Sharp, J.M., 2004. How can SMEs effectively implement the CSR agenda? A UK case study perspective. Corporate Social Responsibility & Environmental Management 11, 140–149.

Ciliberti, F., Pontrandolfo, P., Scozzi, B., 2008. Investigating corporate social responsibility in supply chains: a SME perspective. Journal of Cleaner Production 16, 1579–1588. doi:10.1016/j.jclepro.2008.04.016

Crane, A., McWilliams, A., Matten, D., Moon, Siegel, D. (Eds.), 2008. The Oxford handbook of corporate social responsibility. Oxford University Press, Oxford; New York.

Cummings, B., 2012. BENEFIT CORPORATIONS: HOW TO ENFORCE A MANDATE TO PROMOTE THE PUBLIC INTEREST. Columbia Law Review 112, 578.

Dahlsrud, A., 2008. How corporate social responsibility is defined: an analysis of 37 definitions. Corporate Social Responsibility and Environmental Management 15, 1–13. doi:10.1002/csr.132

Denscombe, M., 2007. The good research guide: for small.scale social research, 3rd Edition. ed. Open University Press, Buckingham.

Denzin, N.K., 1983. Interpretive Interactionism, in: Morgan, G. (Ed.), Beyond Method: Strategies for Social Research. Sage, Beverly Hills, CA, USA.

Denzin, N.K., 1970. The Research Act in Sociology. Butterworth, London.

Die WELT, 1995. Proteste gegen Shell weiten sich aus - Nachrichten DIE WELT - DIE WELT [WWW Document]. Die Welt. URL http://www.welt.de/print-welt/article659638/Proteste-gegen-Shell-weiten-sich-aus.html (accessed 2.16.13).

Du, S., Bhattacharya, C.B., Sen, S., 2011. Corporate Social Responsibility and Competitive Advantage: Overcoming the Trust Barrier. Management Science 57, 1528–1545.

Du, S., Bhattacharya, C.B., Sen, S., 2010. Maximizing Business Returns to Corporate Social Responsibility (CSR): The Role of CSR Communication. International Journal of Management Reviews 12, 8–19.

Duan, H., Han, X., Yang, H., 2009. An Analysis of Causes for SMEs Financing Difficulty. International Journal of Business and Management 4, P73.

Durmaz, V., Ateş, S.S., Duman, G., 2011. CSR As A Tool To Cope With Economic Crises: The Case Of TEI. Procedia - Social and Behavioral Sciences 24, 1418–1426. doi:10.1016/j.sbspro.2011.09.098

Elkington, J., Fennell, S., 2000. Partners for Sustainability, in: Bendell, J. (Ed.), Terms for Endearment: Business, NGOs and Sustainable Development. Greenleaf, Sheffield, pp. 150–162.

Engels, F., 2009. The condition of the working class in England, Oxford world's classics. Oxford University Press, Oxford ; New York.

European Commission, 2013a. Corporate Social Responsibility and Small & Medium Enterprises (SMEs) - Corporate social responsibility - Enterprise and Industry [WWW Document]. European Commission. URL http://ec.europa.eu/enterprise/policies/sustainable-business/corporate-social-responsibility/sme/ (accessed 6.12.13).

European Commission, 2013b. Corporate Social Responsibility and Small & Medium Enterprises (SMEs) - Corporate social responsibility - Enterprise and Industry [WWW Document]. URL http://ec.europa.eu/enterprise/policies/sustainable-business/corporate-social-responsibility/sme/ (accessed 7.24.13).

European Commission, 2005. The new SME definition: user guide and model declaration, Enterprise and industry publications. Office for Official Publications of the European Communities, Luxembourg.

European Commission, 2002. SMEs in Europe: competitiveness, innovation and the knowledge-driven society, data 1996-2001. Office for Official Publications of the European Communities, Luxembourg.

Federation of Small businesses, 2013. Small Business Statistics [WWW Document]. Federation of Small Businesses. URL http://www.fsb.org.uk/stats (accessed 5.31.13).

Forum Europe, 2012. Policies & Practices | How to integrate adapted CSR policies in SMEs? [WWW Document]. policies & practices. URL http://www.eu-ems.com/practical.asp?event_id=119&page_id=1139 (accessed 3.14.13).

Friedman, M., 1972. Milton Friedman Responds. Business and Society Review 1, 5–16.

Garside, J., 2012. Apple's factories in China are breaking employment laws, audit finds [WWW Document]. The Guardian. URL http://www.guardian.co.uk/technology/2012/mar/30/apple-factories-china-foxconn-audit (accessed 2.26.13).

Gjolberg, M., 2009. The origin of corporate social responsibility: global forces or national legacies? Socio-Economic Review 7, 605–637. doi:10.1093/ser/mwp017

Goddard, W., Melville, S., 2004. Research methodology: an introduction, 2nd Edition. ed. Juta, Lansdowne.

Gomm, R., 2004. Social Research Methodology. A critical introduction. Palgrave Macmillan, Hampshire.

Goosen, R., 2009. Focus on CSR as a Competitive Advantage [WWW Document]. Make Good. URL http://www.makegood.com/blog/2009/09/04/focus-on-csr-as-a-competitive-advantage/ (accessed 2.24.13).

Grollmann, D., 1996. "--für tüchtige Meister und Arbeiter rechter Art": Eisenheim, die älteste Arbeitersiedlung im Ruhrgebiet macht Geschichte, Schriften / Rheinischen Industriemuseums. Rheinland, Köln.

Haralambos, M., Holborn, M., 2008. Sociology: themes and perspectives, 7th e. ed. Collins, London.

Henshaw, L., 2011. How SMEs can engage in social responsibility programmes [WWW Document]. The Guardian. URL http://www.guardian.co.uk/voluntary-sector-network/community-action-blog/2011/dec/05/corporate-social-responsibility-daunting (accessed 3.14.13).

Holme, R., Watts, P., 2000. Corporate social responsibility: making good business sense. World Business Council for Sustainable Development, Conches-Geneva, Switzerland.

Karnani, A., 2007. Fortune at the Bottom of the Pyramid: A Mirage. California Management Review, Forthcoming.

Kechiche, A., Soparnot, R., 2012. CSR within SMEs: Literature Review. International Business Research 5, 97.

Klein, P., 2011. Three Great Examples of Shared Value in Action - Forbes [WWW Document]. Forbes. URL http://www.forbes.com/sites/csr/2011/06/14/three-great-examples-of-shared-value-in-action/ (accessed 6.10.13).

Kotey, B., Meredith, G.G., 1997. Relationships among owner/manager personal values, business strategies and enterprise performance. Journal of Small Business Management 35, 37–64.

Lawrence, F., 2013. Horsemeat scandal: fear that culprits will not face justice [WWW Document]. The Guardian. URL http://www.guardian.co.uk/uk/2013/may/10/horsemeat-scandal-fear-culprits-justice (accessed 5.27.13).

Lepoutre, J., Heene, A., 2006. Investigating the Impact of Firm Size on Small Business Social Responsibility: A Critical Review. Journal of Business Ethics 67, 257–273.

Levitt, T., 1958. The Dangers of Social Responsibility. Harvard Business Review 36, 41–50.

MARS, 2013. Cocoa Sustainability | Securing Cocoa's Future | Mars [WWW Document]. MARS. URL http://www.mars.com/global/brands/cocoa-sustainability-home.aspx (accessed 6.1.13).

Marshall, M.N., 1996. Sampling for qualitative research. Family practice 13, 522–526.

McWilliams, A., Siegel, D.S., Wright, P.M., 2006. Corporate Social Responsibility: Strategic Implications*. Journal of Management Studies 43, 1–18. doi:10.1111/j.1467-6486.2006.00580.x

Midttun, A., Gautesen, K., Gjølberg, M., 2006. The political economy of CSR in Western Europe. Corporate Governance 6, 369–385. doi:10.1108/14720700610689496

Müller, M., Schaltegger, S. (Eds.), 2008. Corporate Social Responsibility: Trend oder Modeerscheinung? : ein Sammelband mit ausgewählten Beiträgen von Mitgliedern des Doktorandennetzwerkes Nachhaltiges Wirtschaften (DNW). Oekom-Verl., München.

Neck, H.M., Zacharakis, A.L., Bygrave, W.D., Reynolds, P.D., 2003. Global Entrepreneurship Monitor.

Nestle, 2013. What is Creating Shared Value | Nestlé Global [WWW Document]. Nestle. URL http://www.nestle.com/csv/what-is-csv (accessed 6.1.13).

Nestle, 2012a. Nestle Full CSV Report.

Nestle, 2012b. Working with dairy farmers [WWW Document]. Nestle. URL http://www.nestle.com/brands/dairy/dairycsv (accessed 6.1.13).

Neumann, W.L., 2003. Social research methods: Qualitative and quantitative approaches, 5th edition. ed. Allyn & Bacon, Boston.

Newell, P., 2000. Globalisation and the New Politics of Sustainable Development, in: Bendell, J. (Ed.), Terms for Endearment: Business, NGOs and Sustainable Development. Greenleaf, Sheffield, pp. 31–39.

Nooteboom, B., 1993. Firm size effects on transaction costs. Small Business Economics 5, 283–295.

Onwuegbuzie, A.J., 2000. Positivists, post-positivists, post-structuralists, and post-modernists: Why can't we all get along? Towards a framework for unifying research paradigms.

Presented at the Annual meeting of the Association for the Advancement of Educational Research, Ponte Vedra, FL, USA.

Patton, M.Q., 2002. Qualitative research and evaluation methods, 3 ed. ed. Sage Publications, Thousand Oaks, Calif.

Peña, E.D., 2007. Lost in Translation: Methodological Considerations in Cross-Cultural Research. Child Development 78, 1255–1264. doi:10.1111/j.1467-8624.2007.01064.x

Pike, R., 2012. Social License to Operate [WWW Document]. Schroders. URL https://c.na3.content.force.com/servlet/servlet.ImageServer?id=01550000000sKevAAE&oid=00D300000000M2BEAU (accessed 6.6.13).

Porter, M.E., 1991. Towards a dynamic theory of strategy. Strategic Management Journal 12, 95–117. doi:10.1002/smj.4250121008

Porter, M.E., Hills, G., Pfitzer, M., Patscheke, S., Hawkins, E., 2012. Measuring Shared Value. How to unlock value by lining social and business results. FCG.

Porter, M.E., Kramer, M.R., 2011. Creating Shared Value. Harvard Business Review 89, 62–77.

Porter, M.E., Kramer, M.R., 2006. Strategy & Society: The Link Between Competitive Advantage and Corporate Social Responsibility. Harvard Business Review 84, 78–92.

Prahalad, C.K., Hart, S.L., 2002. The Fortune at the Bottom of the Pyramid. Strategy and Business 26, 1–14.

Rappaport, A., 2011. Saving capitalism from short-termism : how to build long-term value and take back our financial future / Alfred Rappaport. New York : McGraw-Hill, c2011.

Santos, M., 2011. CSR in SMEs: strategies, practices, motivations and obstacles. Social Responsibility Journal 7, 490.

Saunders, M., 2009. Research methods for business students, 5th ed. ed. Prentice Hall, New York.

Saunders, M., Lewis, P., Thornhill, A., 2007. Research methods for business students, 4th ed. ed. Financial Times/Prentice Hall, Harlow, England ; New York.

Schofield, J.W., 2002. Increasing the Generalizability of Qualitative Research, in: Huberman, A.M., Miles, M.B. (Eds.), The Qualitative Researcher's Companion. Sage Publications, Thousand Oaks, CA.

Shaw, E., 1999. A guide to the qualitative research process: evidence from a small firm study. Qualitative Market Research: An International Journal 2, 59–70. doi:10.1108/13522759910269973

Silverman, D., 2001. Interpreting qualitative data: methods for analysing talk, text and interaction. Sage, London [u.a.].

Sklair, L., 2001. The transnational capitalist class. Blackwell, Oxford, UK ; Malden, Mass.

Smith, N.C., 2003. Corporate Social Responsibility: WHETHER OR HOW? California Management Review 45, 52–76.

Snyder, M., Swann Jr., W.B., 1978. Behavioral confirmation in social interaction: From social perception to social reality. Journal of Experimental Social Psychology 14, 148–162. doi:10.1016/0022-1031(78)90021-5

Spinelli, E., 2005. The interpreted world: an introduction to phenomenological psychology, 2nd ed. ed. SAGE, London ; Thousand Oaks, Calif.

Steen, M., 2013. Eurozone SMEs struggle to access finance [WWW Document]. Financial Times. URL http://www.ft.com/cms/s/0/a126d3ee-8cd2-11e2-8ee0-00144feabdc0.html#axzz2VjAJgxyb (accessed 6.9.13).

Stoian, C., Ko, W.K., Jarvis, R., Mirkovic, R., 2012. Small and Medium-sized Accountancy Practices Advisory Role in Small and Medium-sized Enterprises' Internationalisation Efforts: An Exploratory Study in the UK [WWW Document]. RAKE Research Projects. URL http://www.isbe.org.uk/RAKE-2012-Research-Projects (accessed 8.15.13).

Supyuenyong, V., Islam, N., Kulkarni, U., 2009. Influence of SME characteristics on knowledge management processes: The case study of enterprise resource planning service providers. Journal of Enterprise Information Management 22, 63–80. doi:10.1108/17410390910922831

Tansky, J.W., Heneman, R., 2003. Guest editor's note: Introduction to the special issue on human resource management in SMEs: A call for more research. Human Resource Management 42, 299–302. doi:10.1002/hrm.10091

TIME Magazine, 2012. Why Companies Can No Longer Afford to Ignore Their Social Responsibilities | TIME.com [WWW Document]. TIME Business and Money. URL http://business.time.com/2012/05/28/why-companies-can-no-longer-afford-to-ignore-their-social-responsibilities/ (accessed 6.12.13).

UN Food and Agricultural Organization, 1990. The community's toolbox: The idea, methods and tools for participatory assessment, monitoring and evaluation in community forestry. [WWW Document]. FAO. URL http://www.fao.org/docrep/x5307e/x5307e08.htm (accessed 7.6.13).

US Census Bureau, 2008. Statistics about Business Size (including Small Business) [WWW Document]. United States Census. URL http://www.census.gov/econ/smallbus.html (accessed 6.9.13).

van Marrewijk, M., 2003. The Concept and Definition of Corporate Social Responsibility. Journal of Business Ethics 44, 95–105.

Visser, W., 2006. Revisiting Carroll's CSR pyramid. Corporate citizenship in developing countries 29–56.

Vogel, D.J., 2005. Is There a Market for Virtue? THE BUSINESS CASE FOR CORPORATE SOCIAL RESPONSIBILITY. California Management Review 47, 19–45.

Vonde, D., 2012. "... dass der Mensch was lernen muss.": Bildungsgeschichte(n) aus dem Ruhrgebiet und dem Bergischen Land. Köndgen, Wuppertal.

Waddel, S., 2000. Complementary Resources: the Win-Win Rationale for Partnerships with NGOs, in: Bendell, J. (Ed.), Terms for Endearment: Business, NGOs and Sustainable Development. Greenleaf, Sheffield, pp. 193–206.

Wilkinson, R.G., Pickett, K., 2010. The spirit level : why equality is better for everyone. Penguin Books, London; New York.

Williams, R., Hayes, J., 2013. Literature review: seminal papers on "Shared value."

Wines, W.A., Napier, N.K., 1992. Toward an Understanding of Cross-Cultural Ethics: A Tentative Model. Journal of Business Ethics 11, 831–841.

Woodcock, N., Green, A., Starkey, M., 2011. Social CRM as a business strategy. Journal of Database Marketing & Customer Strategy Management 18, 50–64. doi:10.1057/dbm.2011.7

Wymenga, P., Spanikova, D.V., Barker A., Konings, D.J., Canton, D.E., 2012. EU SMEs in 2012:at the crossroads. Annual report on small and medium-sized enterprises in the EU, 2011/2012.

www.ingramcontent.com/pod-product-compliance
Lightning Source LLC
Chambersburg PA
CBHW081255180526
45170CB00007B/2433